Unholy Marriage

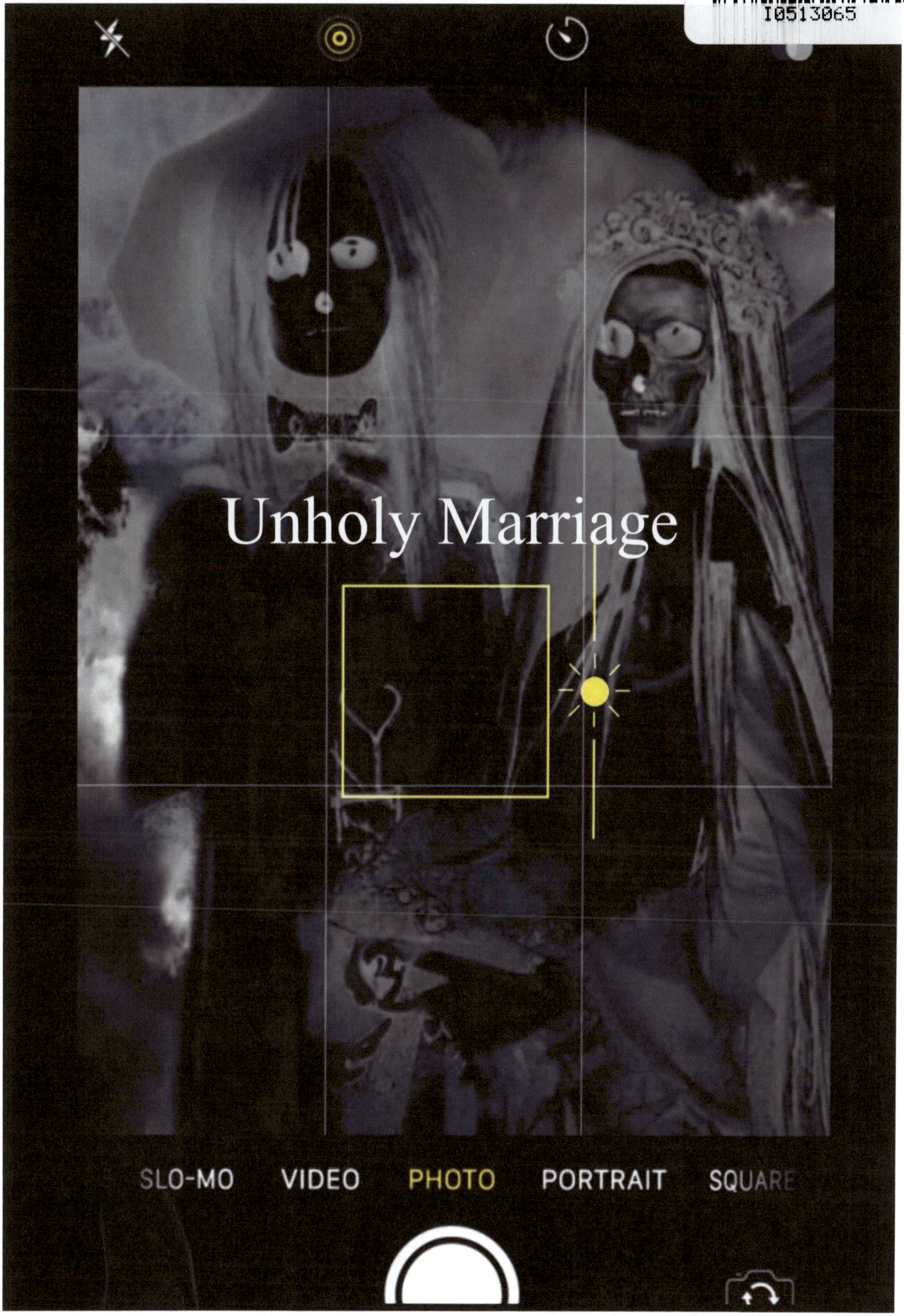

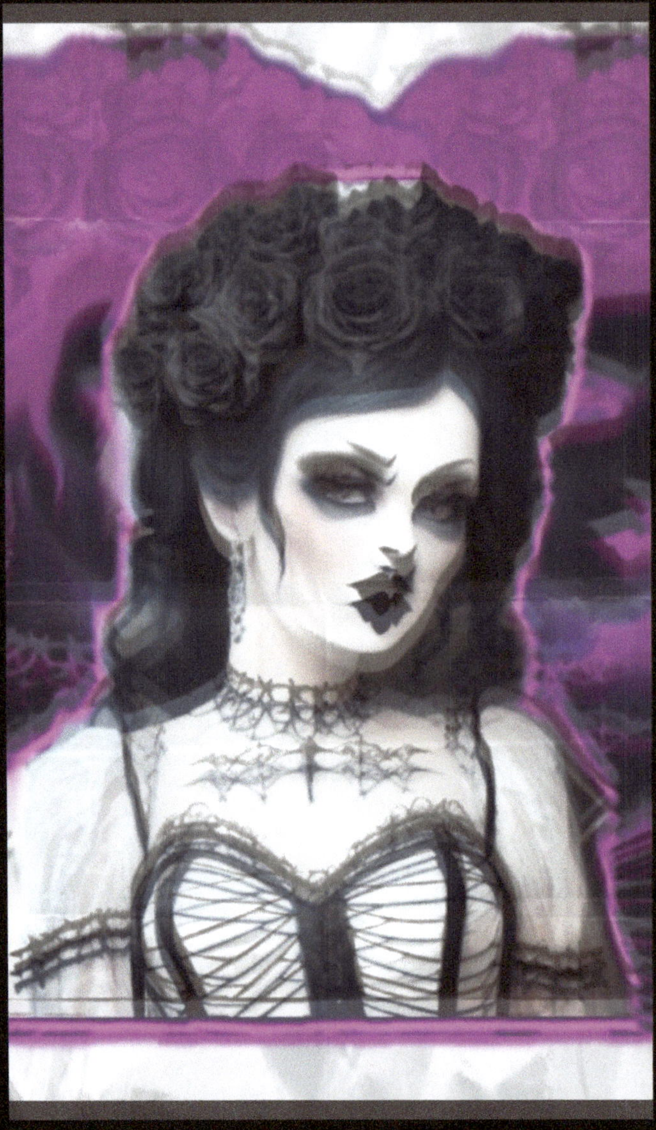

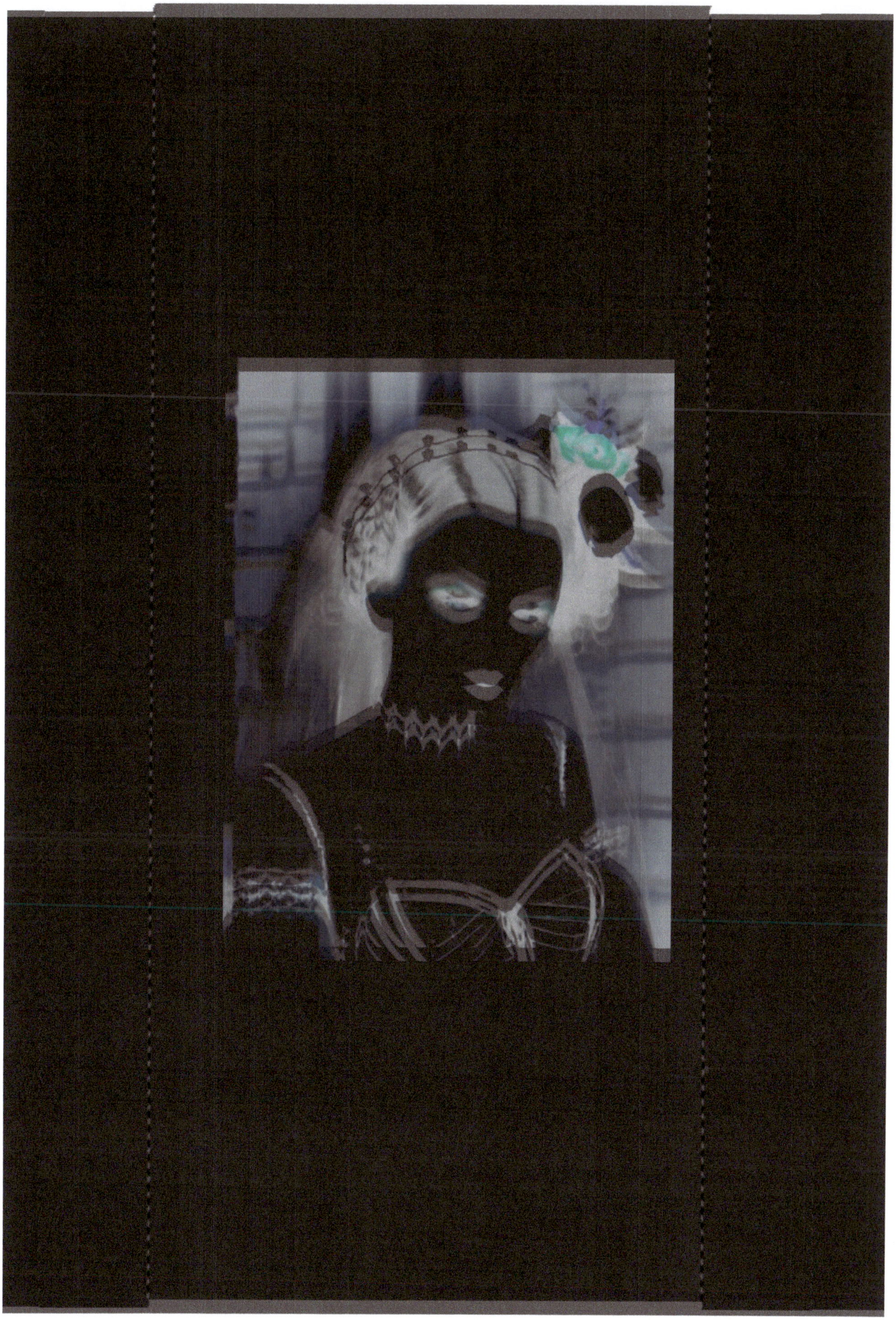

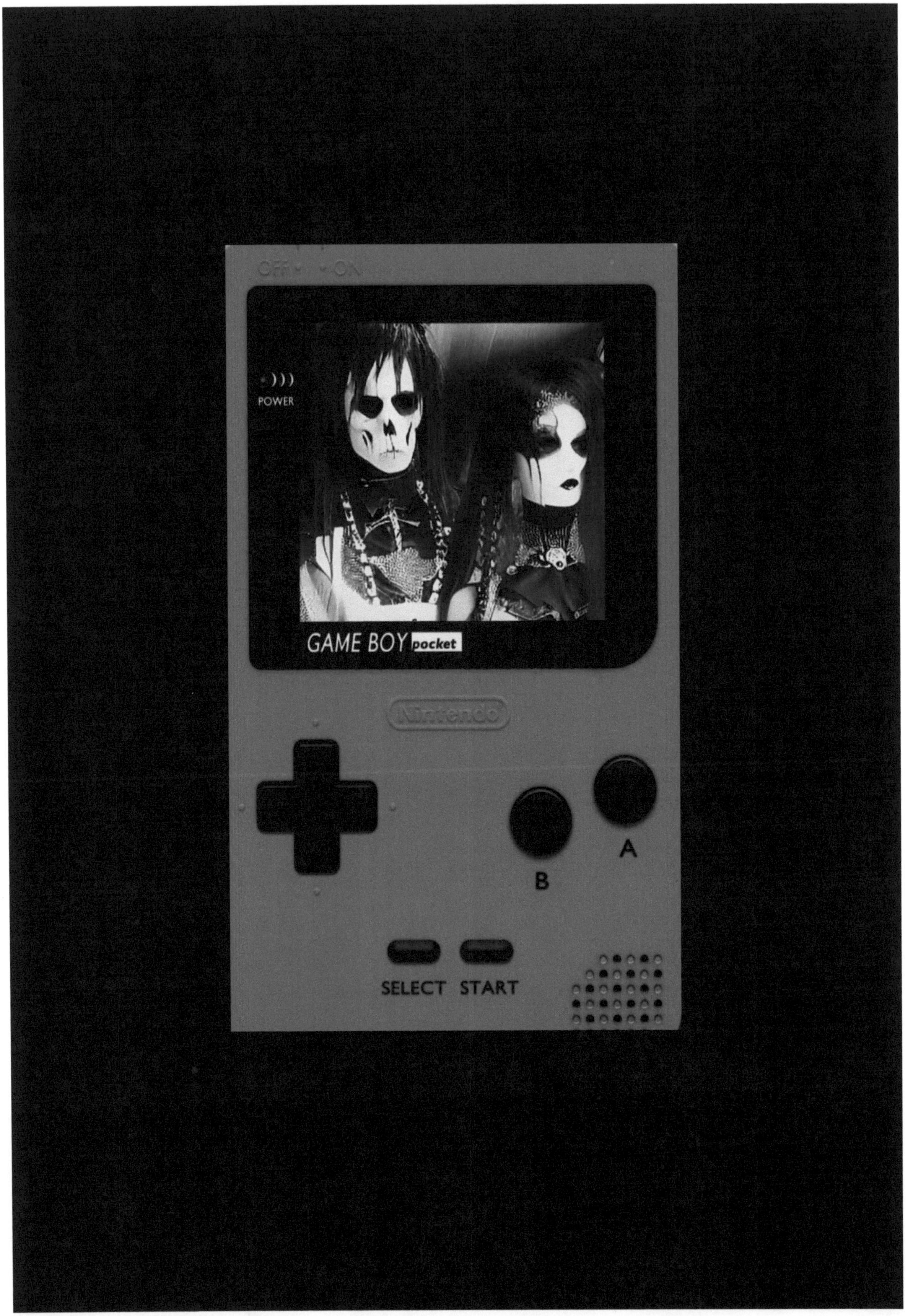
POWER
GAME BOY pocket
Nintendo
B
A
SELECT
START

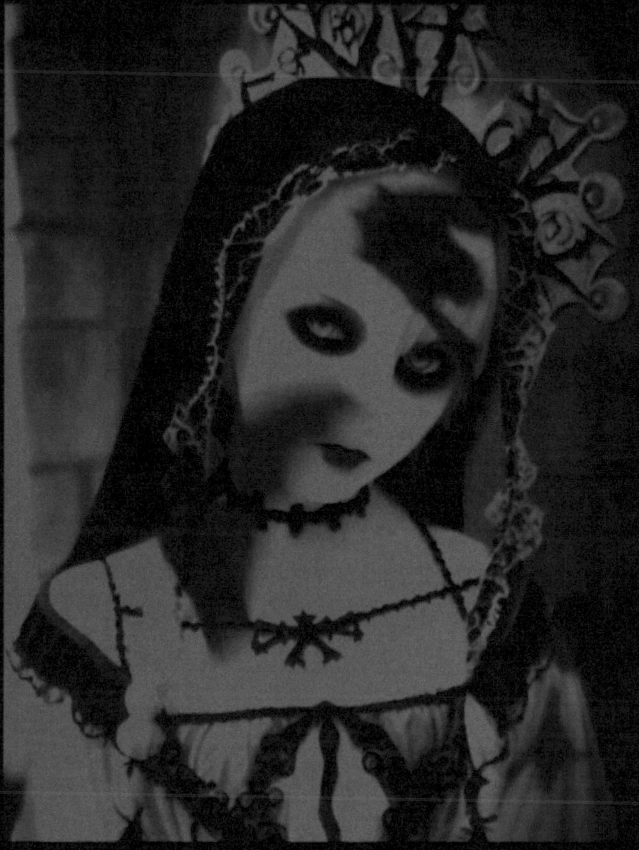

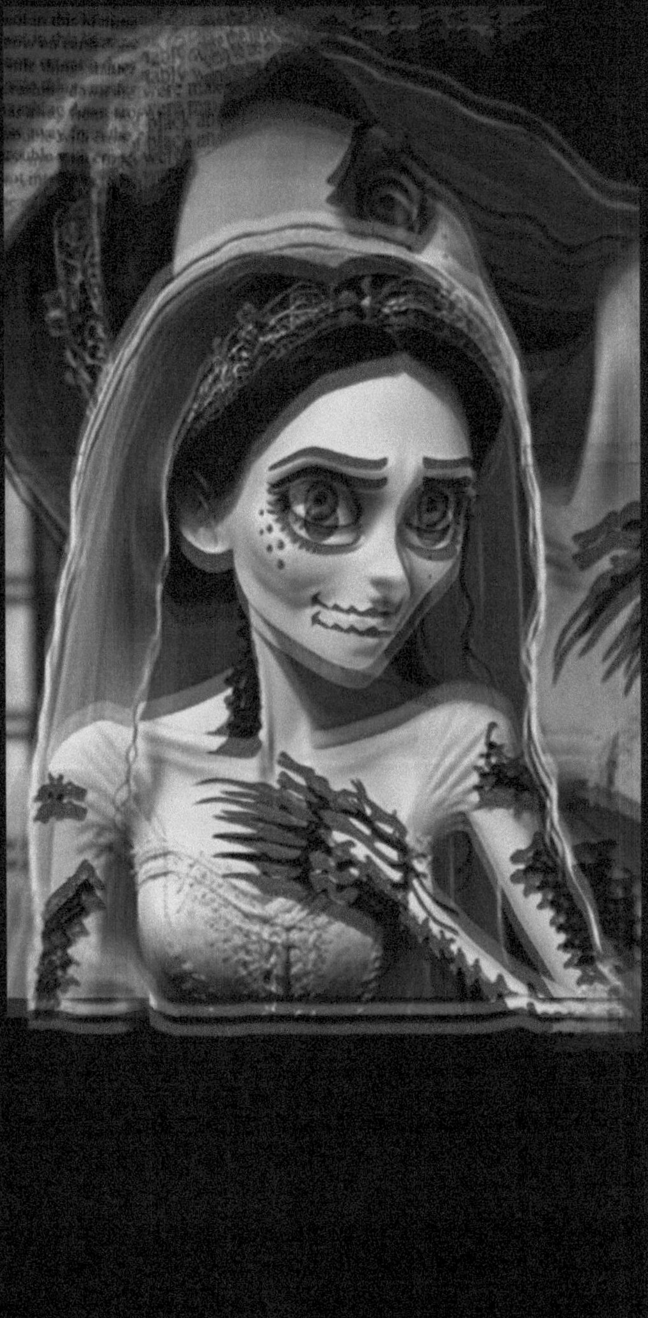

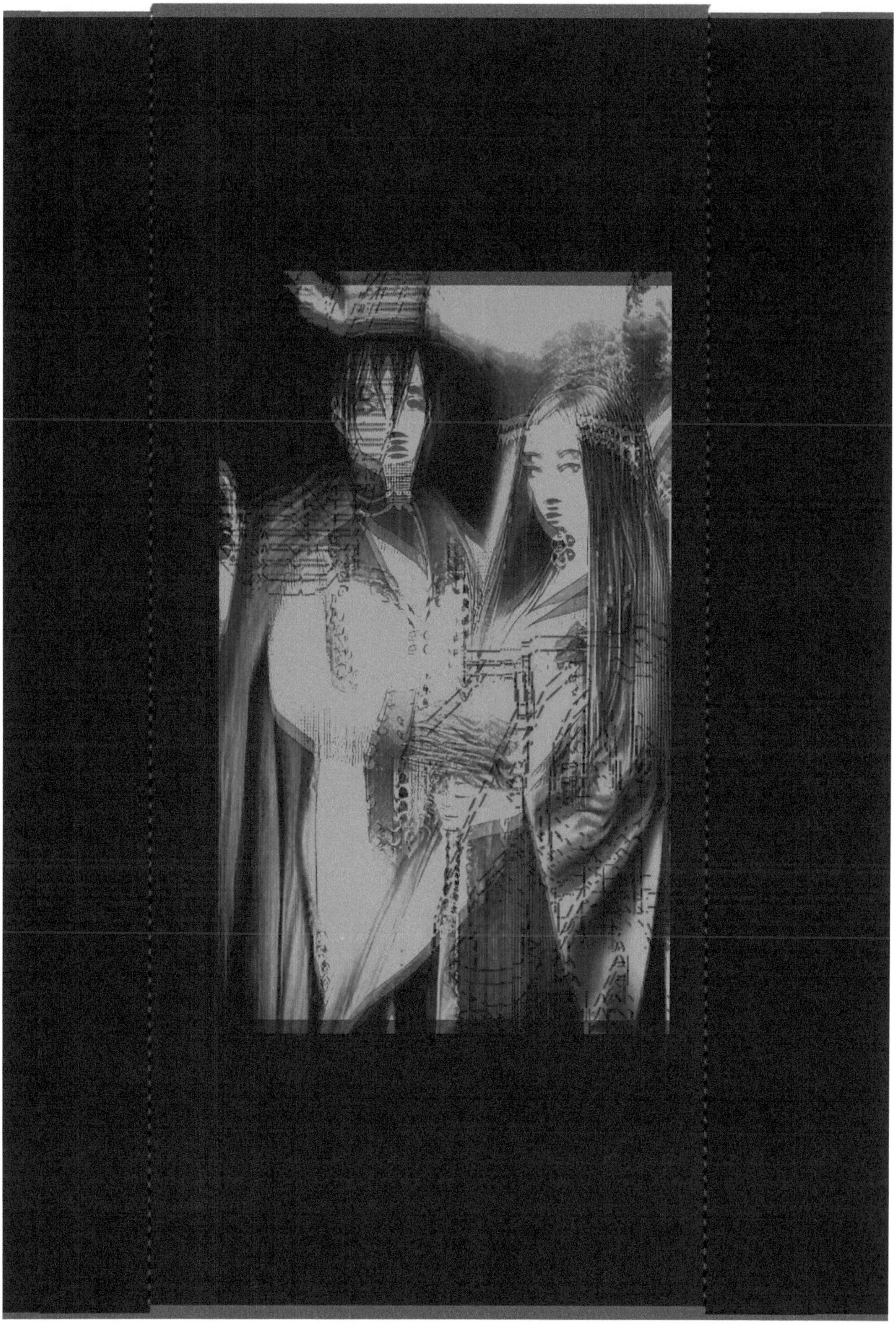

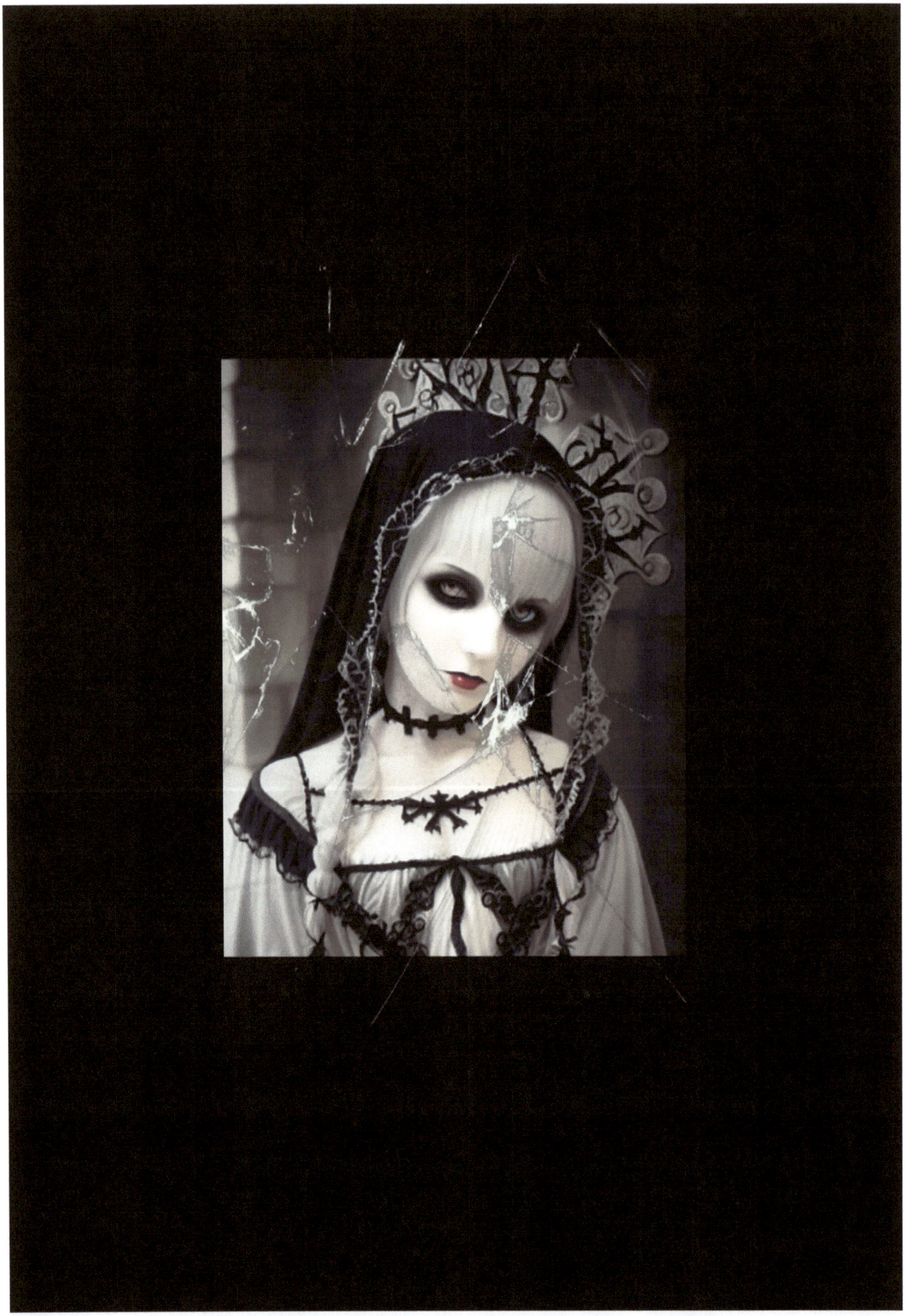

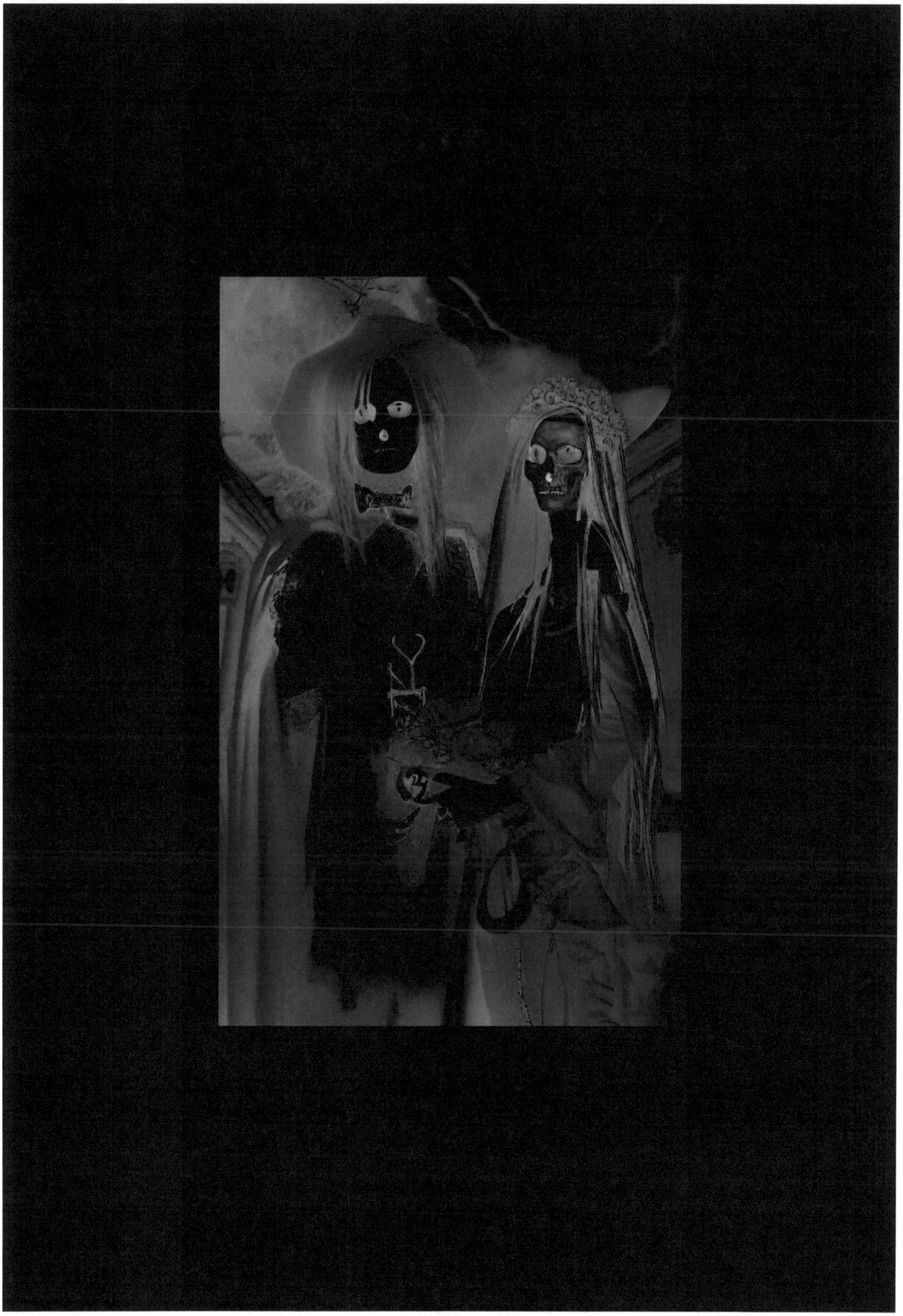

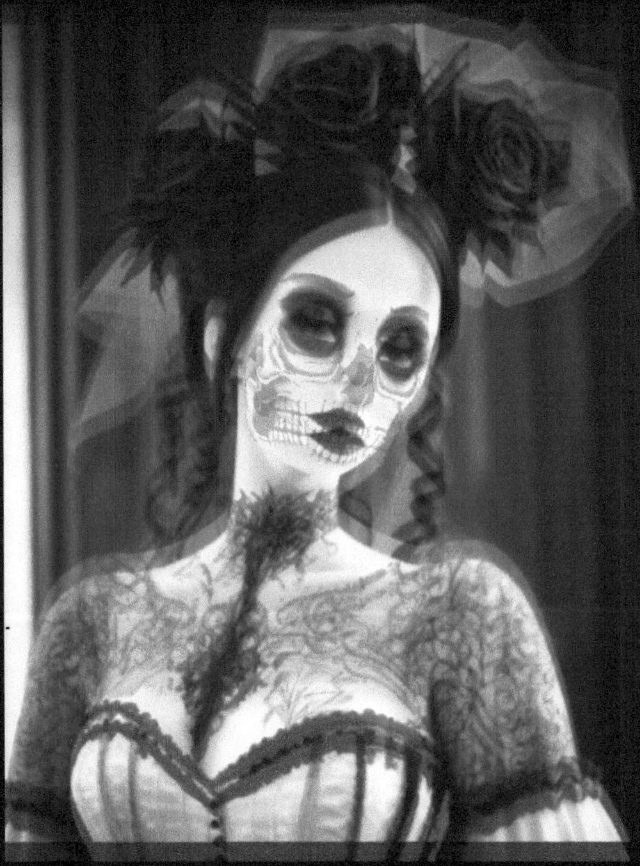

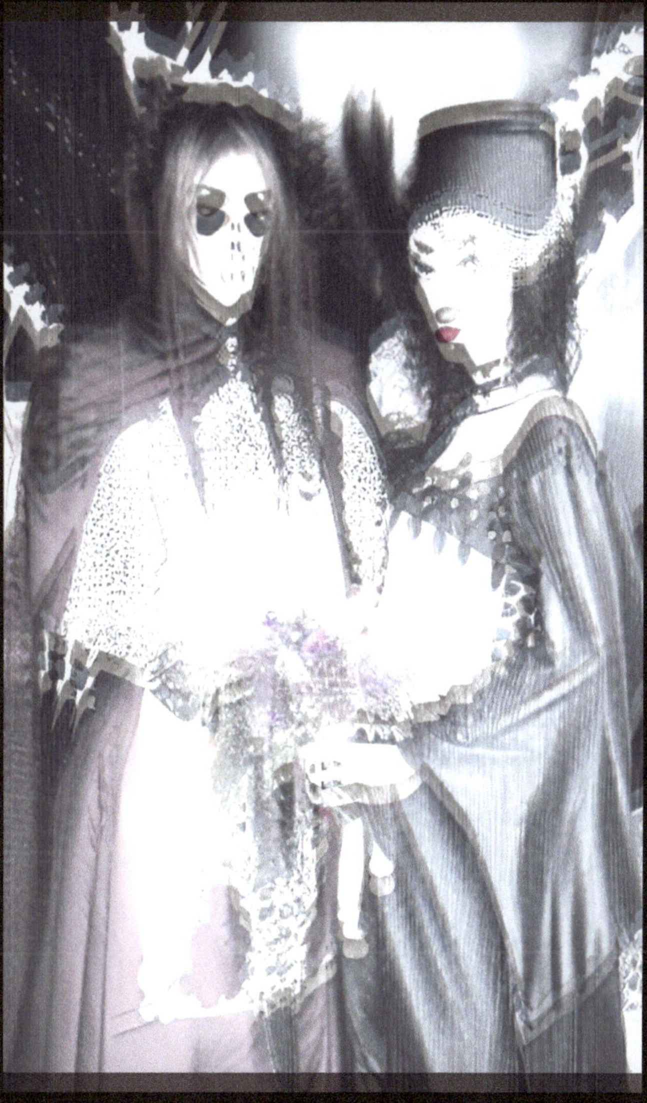

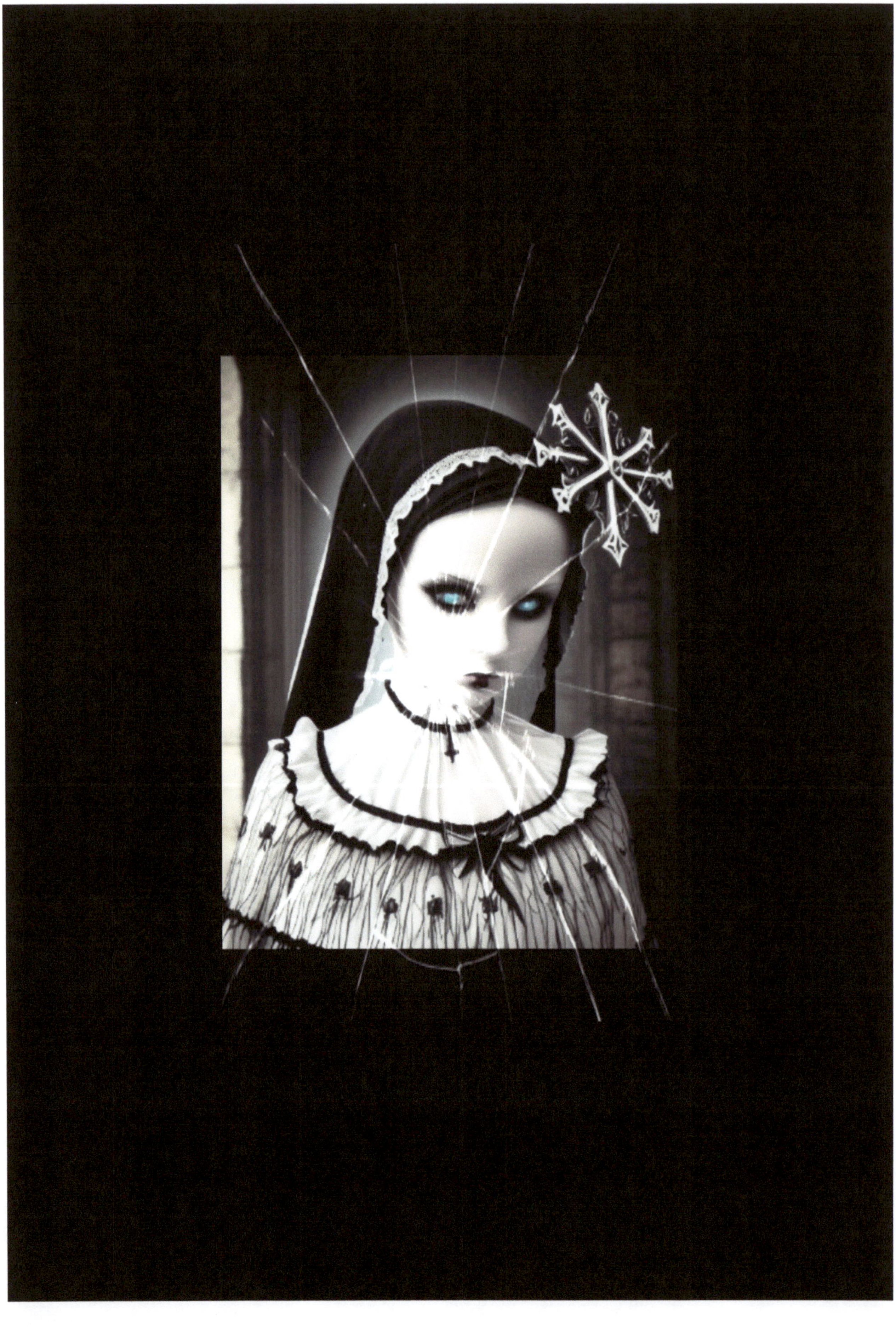

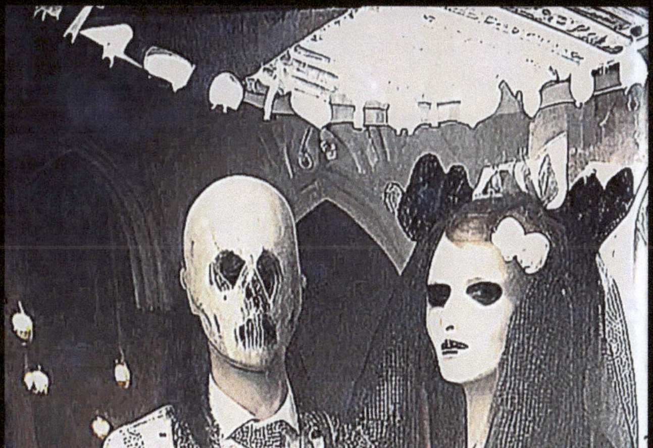

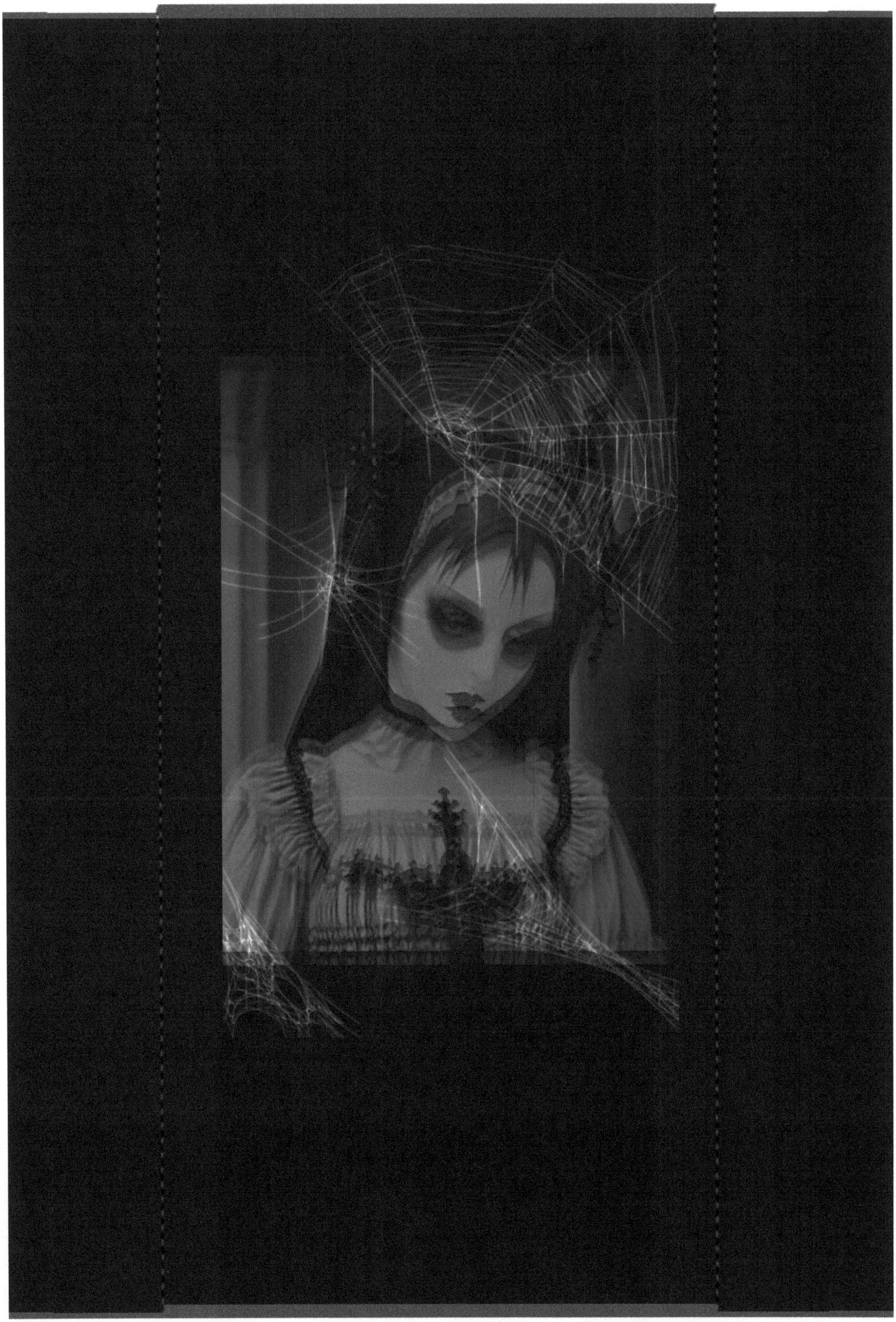

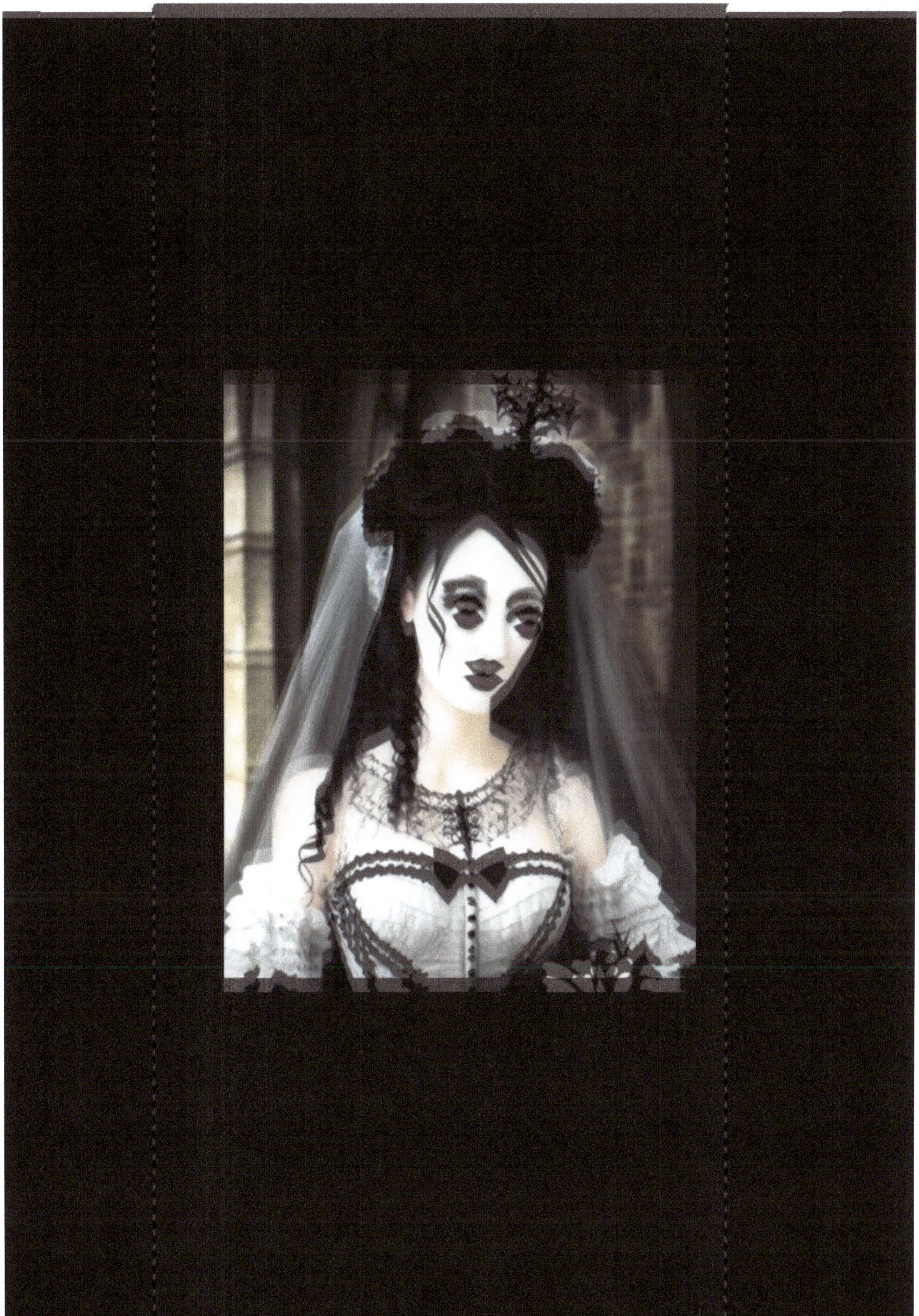

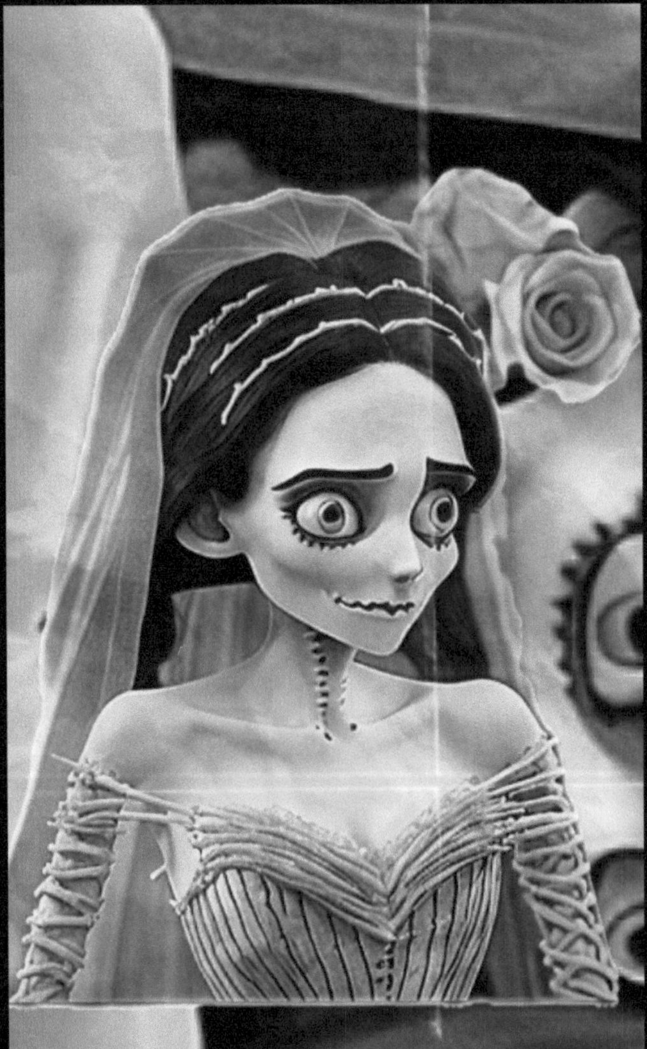

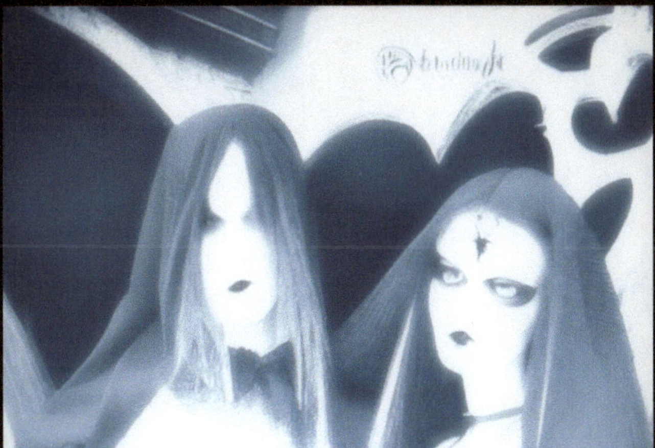

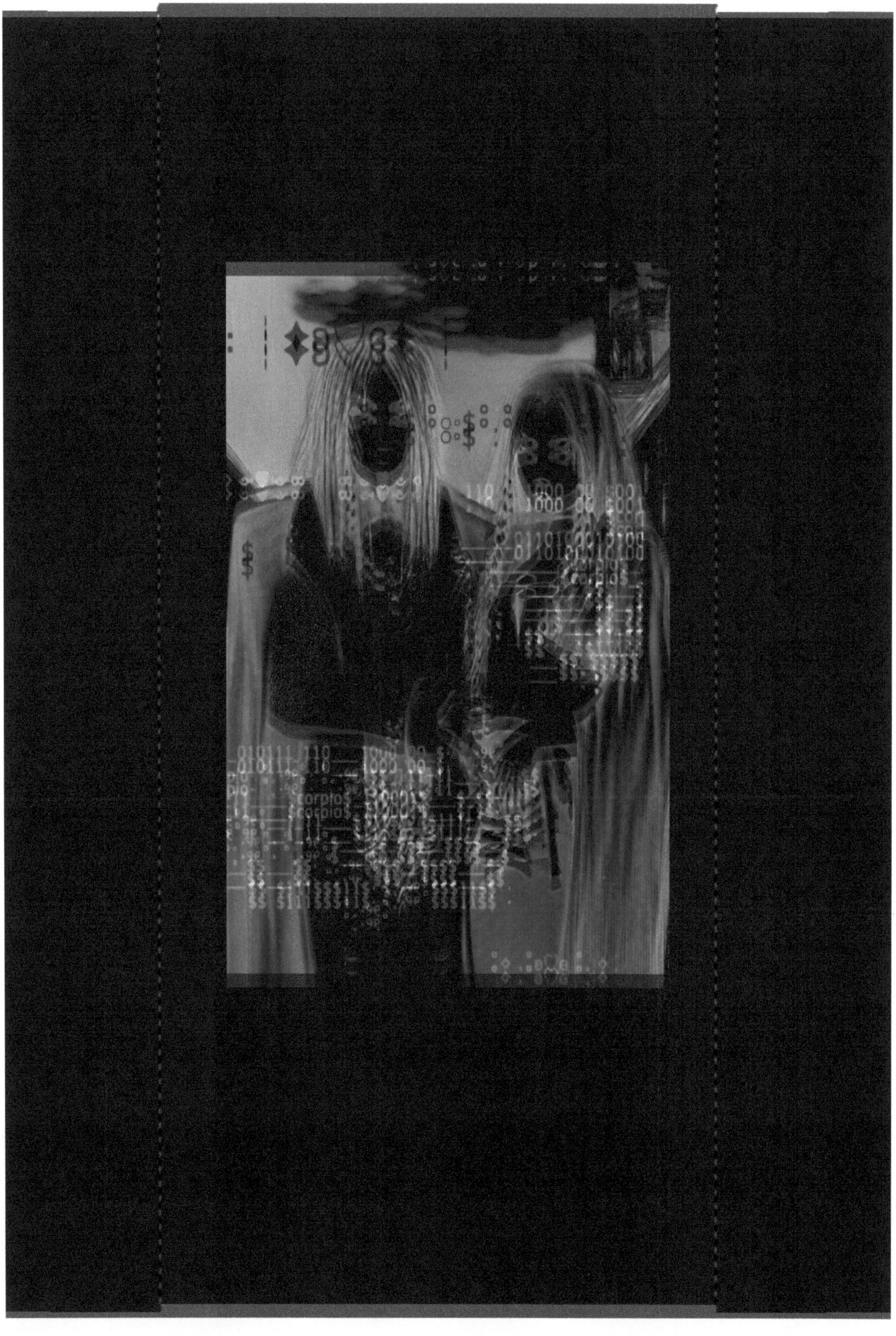

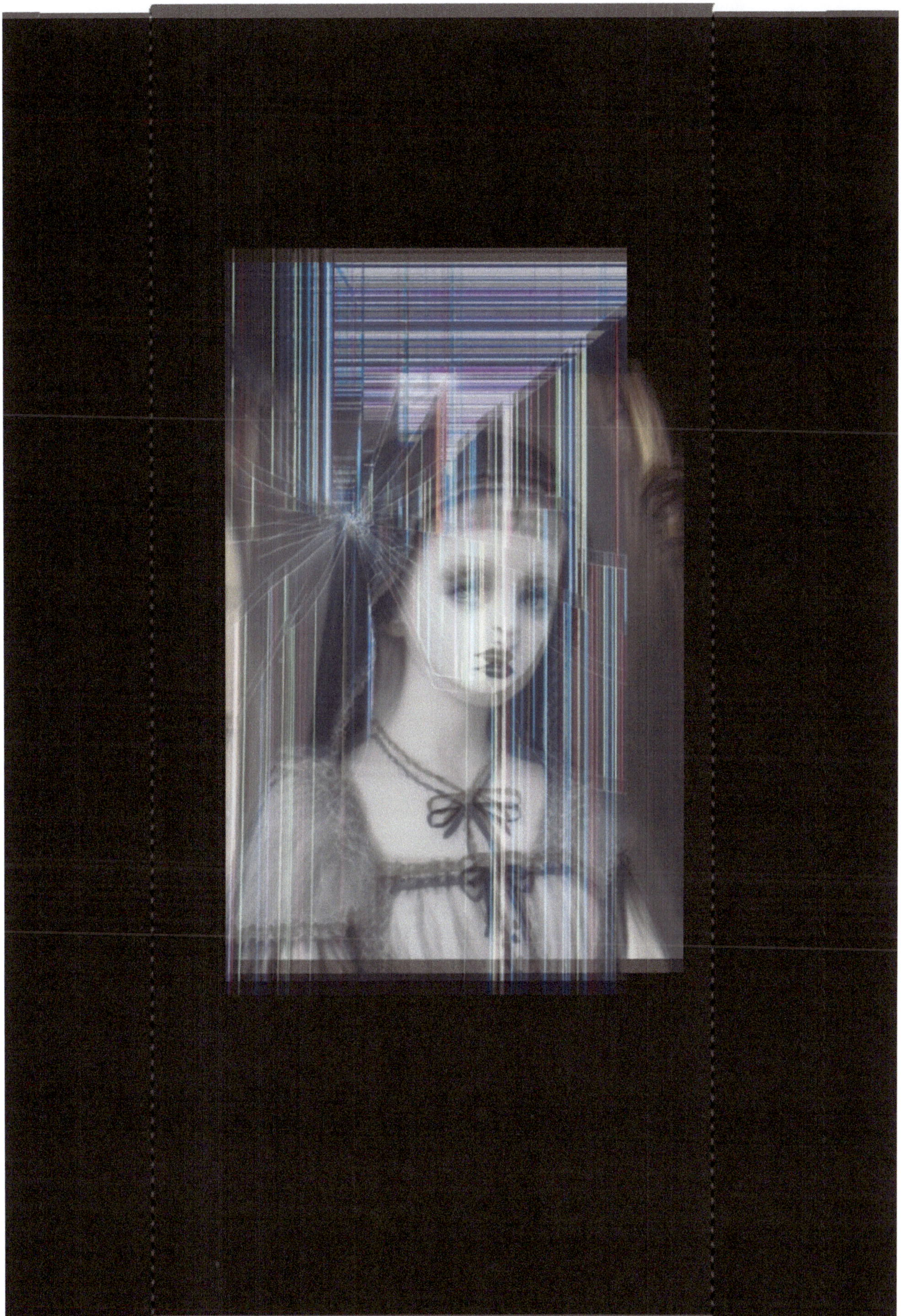

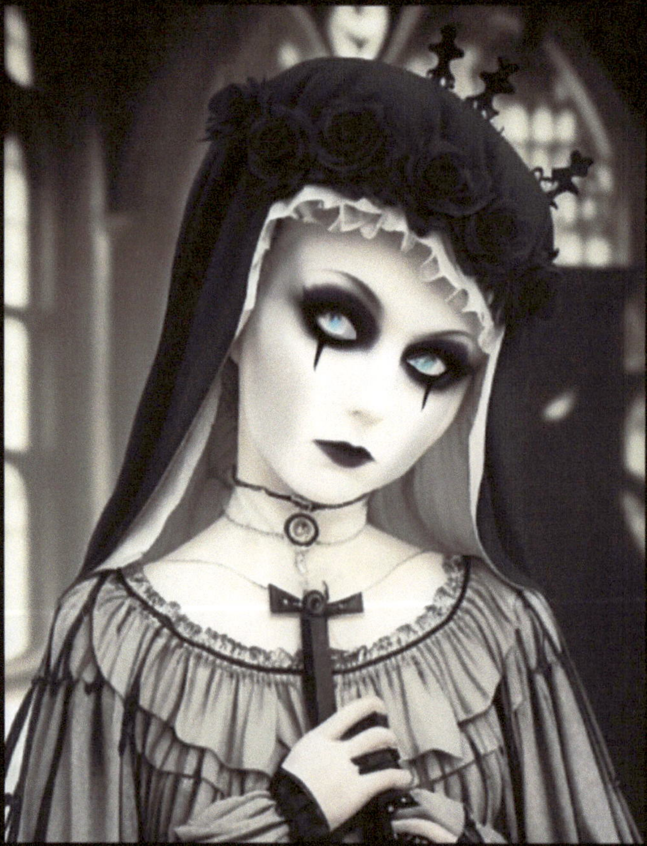

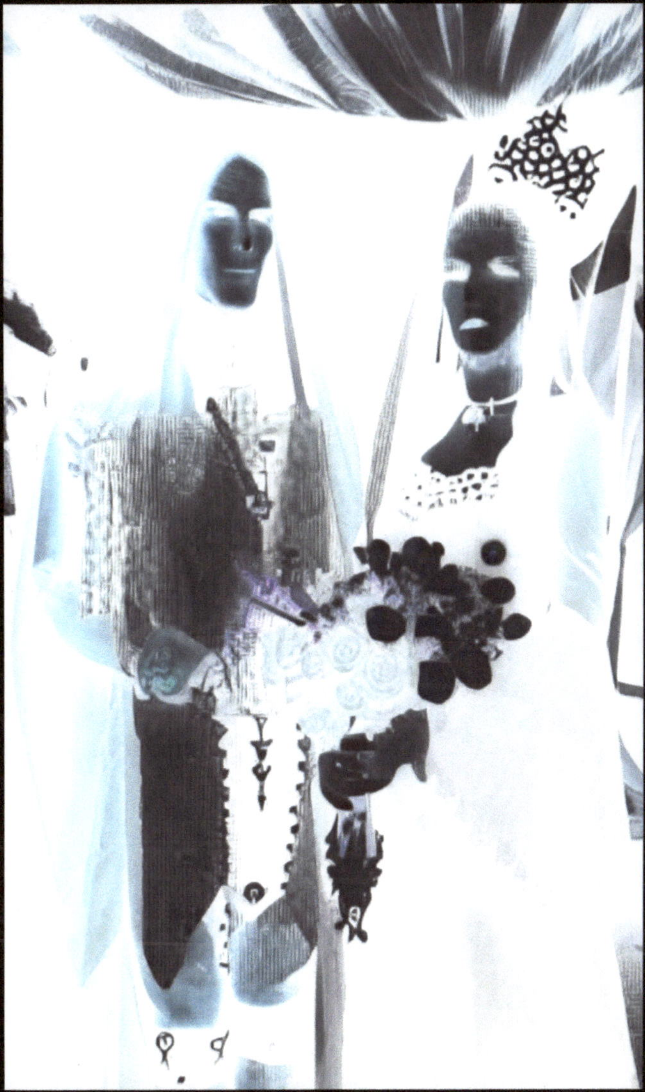

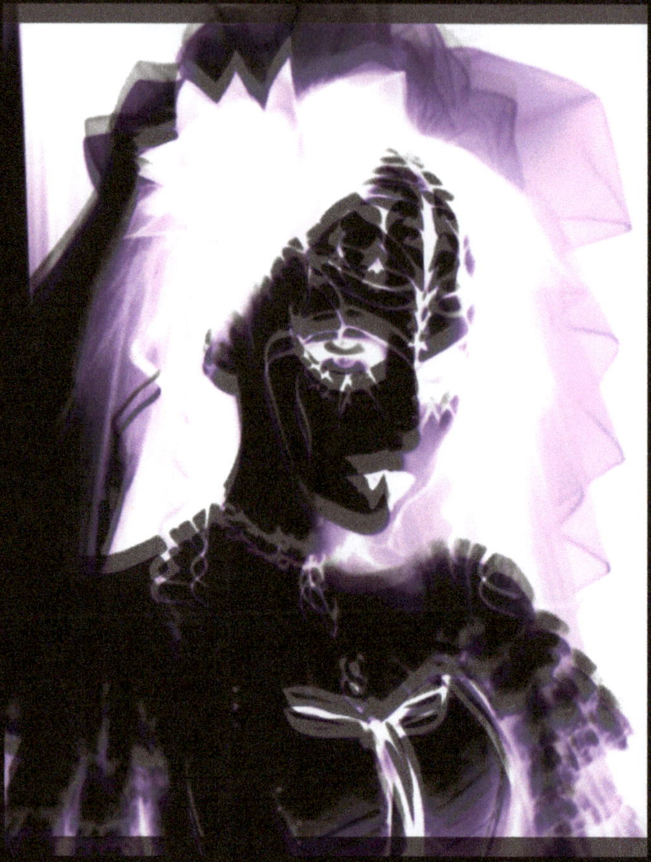

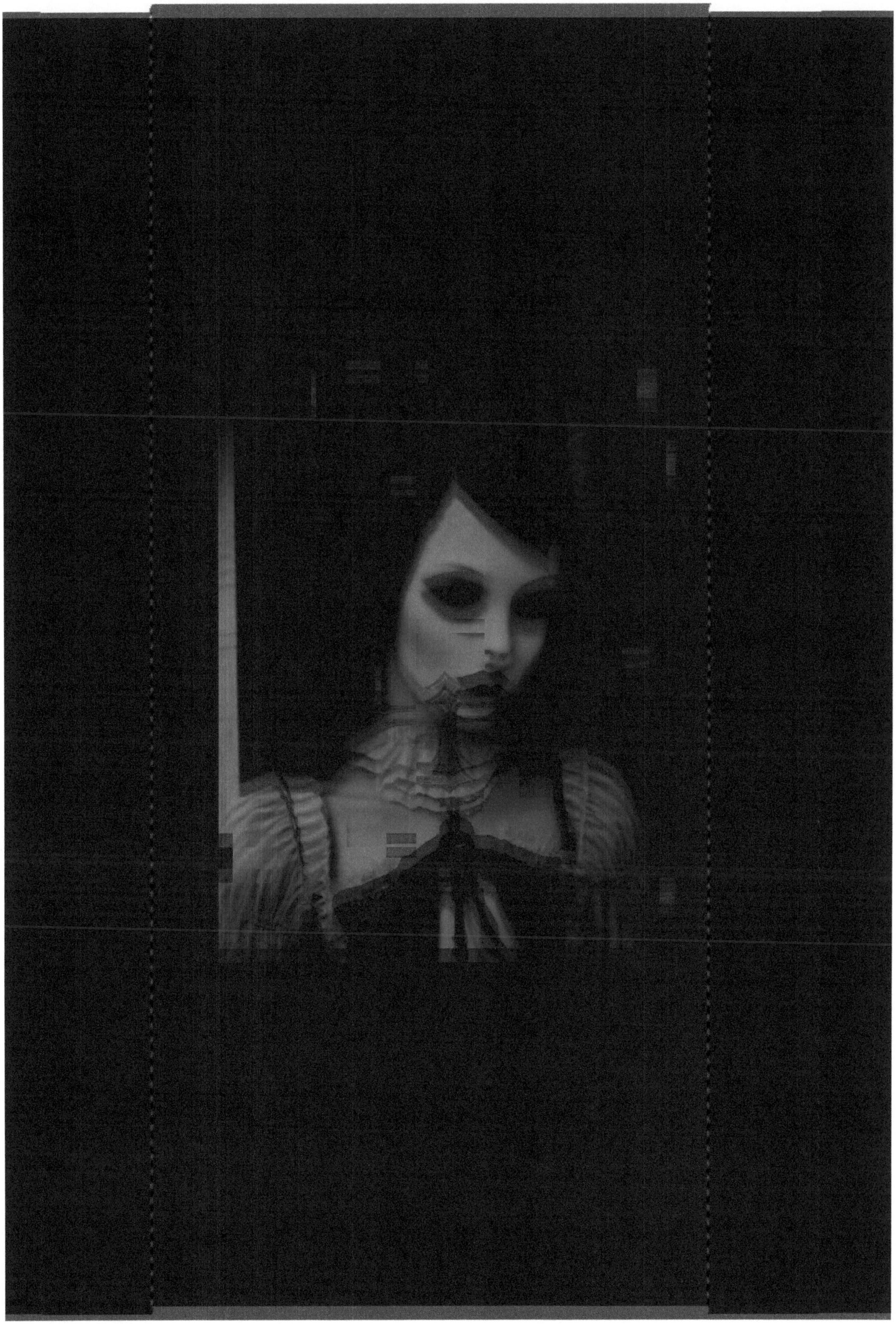

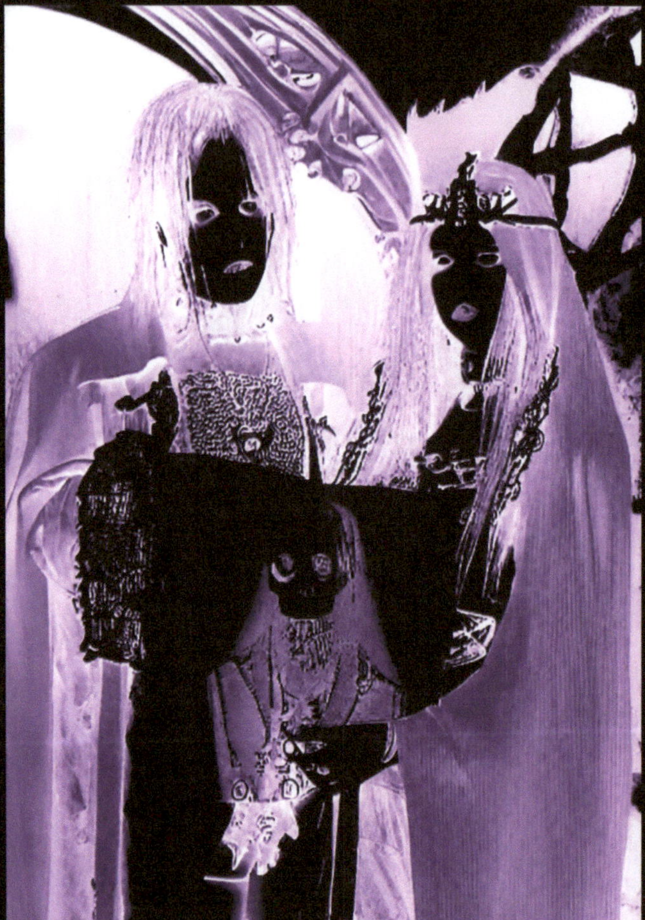

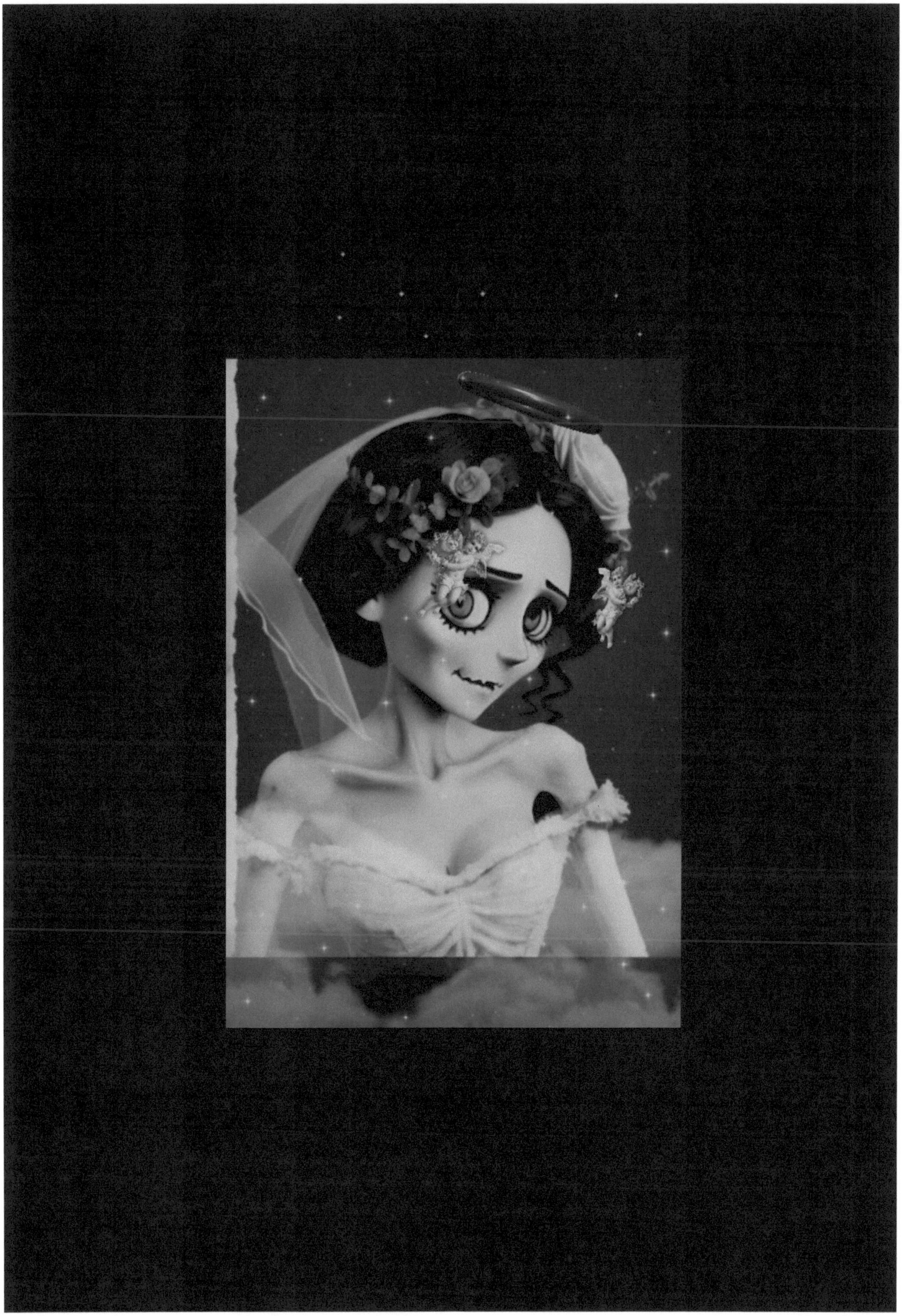

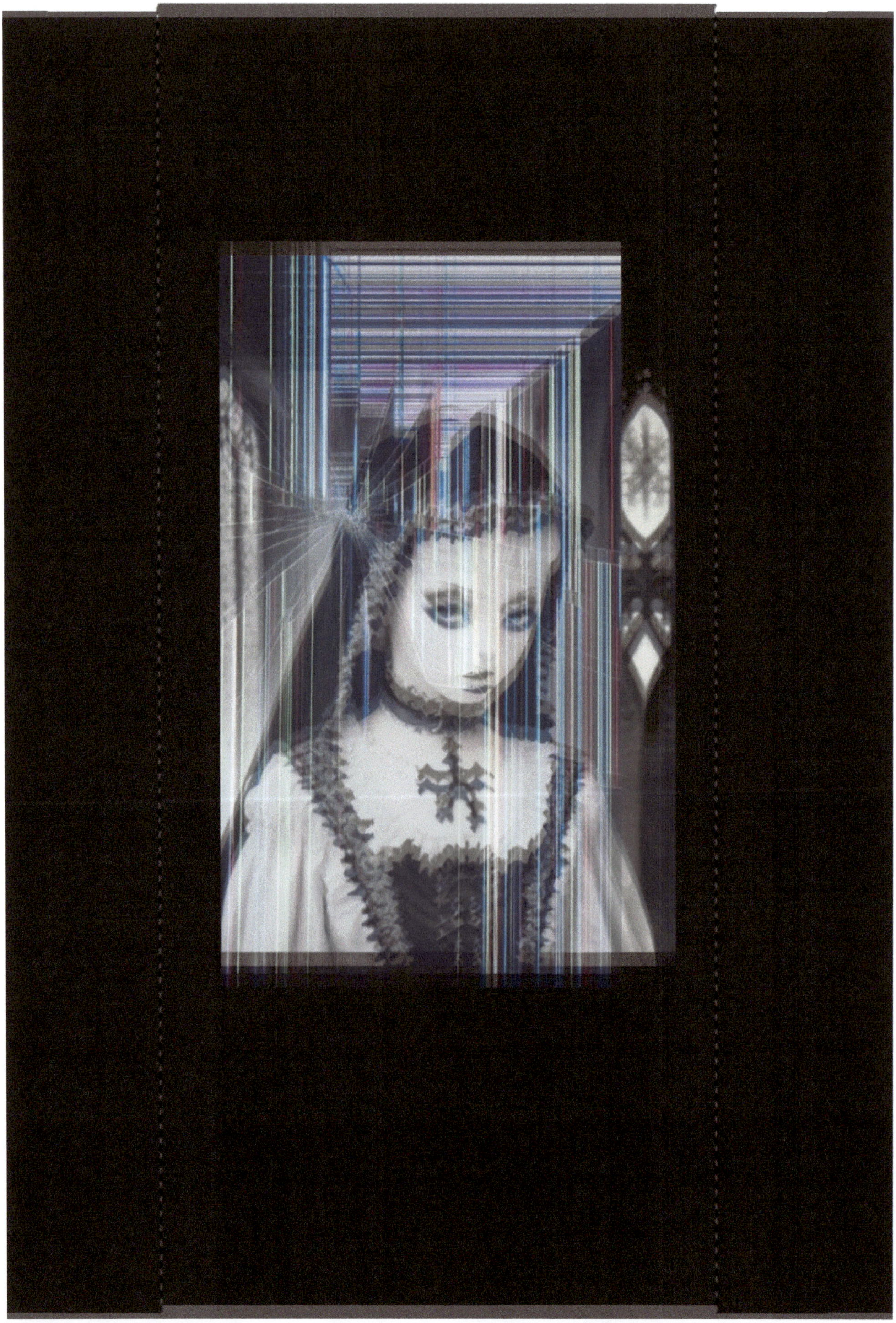

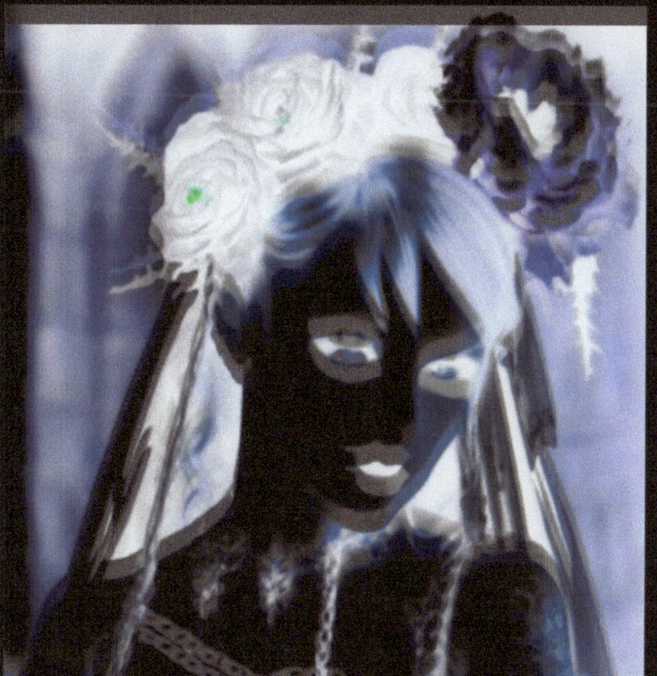

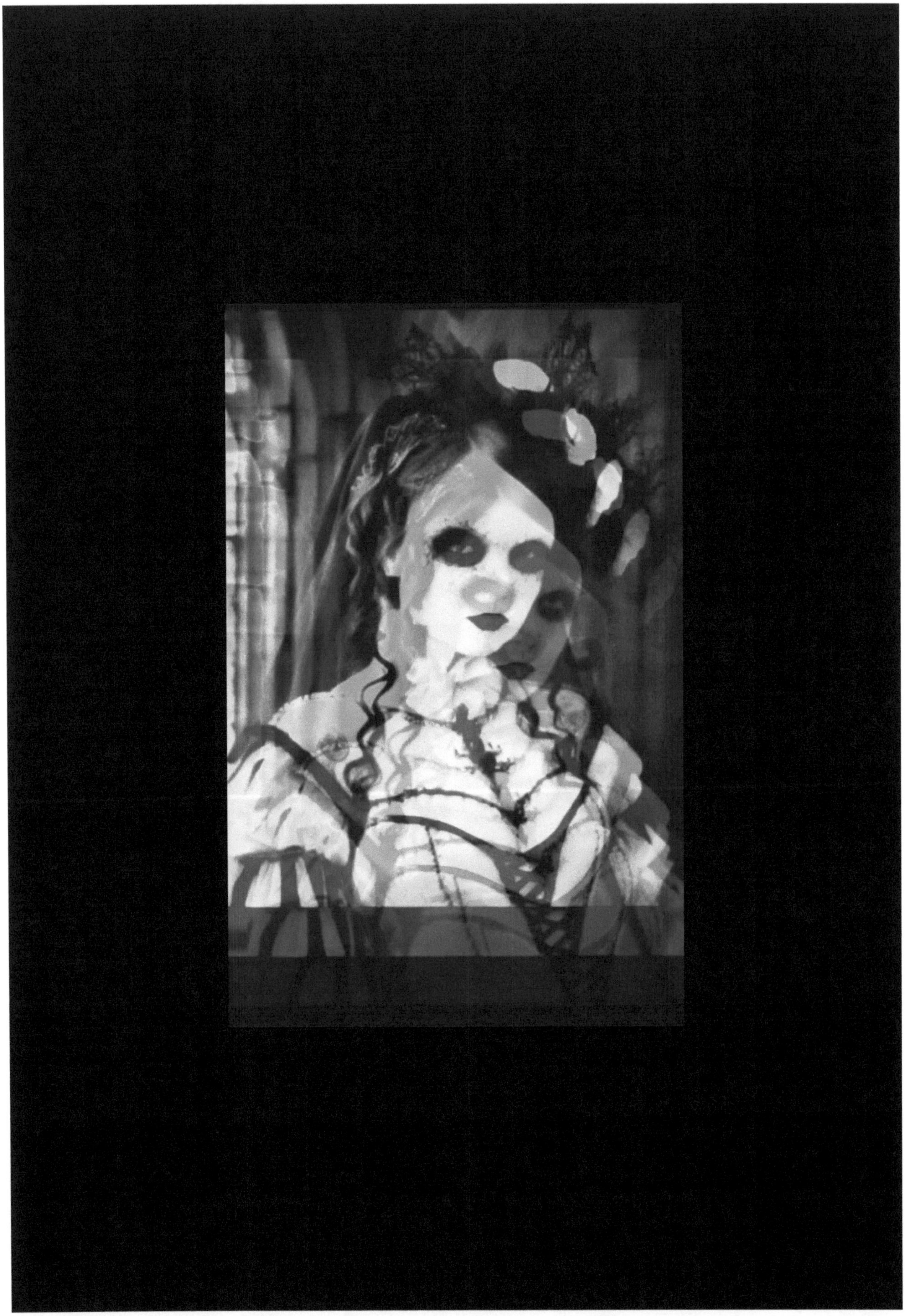

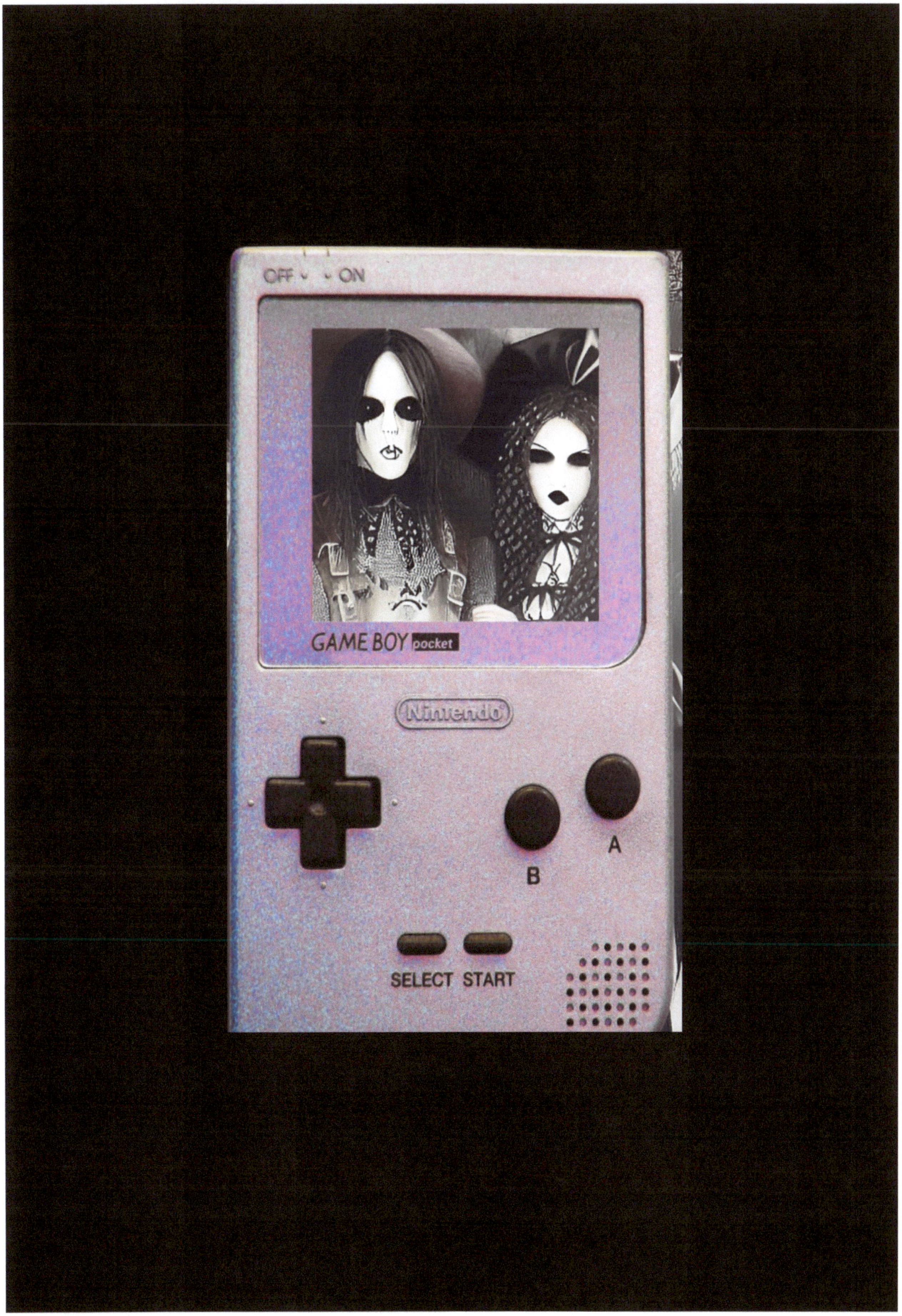
OFF ON
GAME BOY pocket
Nintendo
A
B
SELECT START

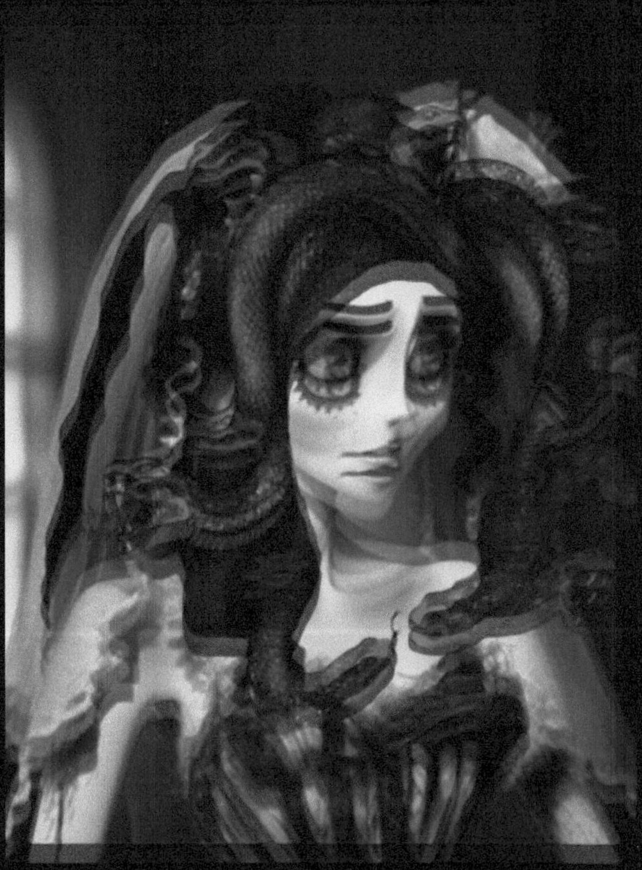

www.ingramcontent.com/pod-product-compliance
Lightning Source LLC
Chambersburg PA
CBHW051954210526
45473CB00030B/2332